Belonging to God

To Bethany, Beth, Rebecca, Charley and Rory

Published by
The Bible Reading Fellowship
Peter's Way, Sandy Lane West
Oxford OX4 5HG
ISBN 1 84101 103 7

First edition 2000
10 9 8 7 6 5 4 3 2 1 0

Acknowledgments
Scripture quotations are taken from the Good News Bible
published by The Bible Societies/HarperCollins*Publishers* Ltd UK
© American Bible Society, 1966, 1971, 1976, 1992.

A catalogue record for this book is available from the British Library.

Printed and bound in Great Britain by Caledonian International
Book Manufacturing Ltd, Glasgow.

Beginning with God

Belonging to God

Exploring the Bible with 5-7s

Rachel Heathfield

A note to parents and carers

This material is to be used ideally with some help. It is designed to help you to talk to your child about God-things and to learn together.

Every session begins with an idea for looking back at the day and thinking of something or someone in particular. That thing or person is then to be prayed for. Encourage your child to voice their prayer, even if it is just a name or word.

The next bit is to enable you to talk together about a topic which will help you to understand what the Bible verse of the day is about. There are no right or wrong answers here, simply ideas to get you thinking on the right lines. Do not be afraid of difficult questions your child might raise; just be as honest as you can.

There is always a suggestion of something to do, which varies from matching up pictures to organizing a time to get up and see the sunrise. This section is deliberately worded so that the activity doesn't have to happen at that moment—particularly if you do the sessions at bed-time! Please support your child by helping him or her to do the activity, and give a reminder of why that activity was suggested.

Explore the Bible is designed to bring together the talking and doing you have just worked through. It might raise more questions, and the answers should be made easier by referring back to the talking bit.

The last part of the session is for the child to complete their own prayer journal on the pages provided. Each session has a linked thought and prayer suggestion. Again, this can be completed straightaway or at another time. Some children might need help; others might like to do it on their own.

I hope you enjoy this material, and may God bless the time you spend with your child exploring the Bible together.

Rachel Heathfield

Children of God

Looking back

What was the best bit of the day just gone?

Say thanks to God for it!

What is coming up that you're looking forward to?

Ask God to be with you.

To talk about

Do you support any teams? Football or rugby, maybe?

Are you in a team?

What is it like to be chosen for a team?

Explore the Bible

Some did receive him and believed in him; so he gave them the right to become God's children.

John 1:12

God promises that when we believe in him we become his child. That doesn't mean we stop being the child of our human parents. It is a bit like becoming part of God's team. As a child of God, we wear God's strip, play God's game and do God's thing!

To do

These teams have their names mixed up!
Can you match the name to the photo?

The Splashing Seven

The Totally Terrific Tumblers

Puddlethwick United

Prayer jotter

God is often called 'Father'. He is the best father we could ever imagine.

Think about the special things your heavenly Father does for you.

Draw or write about them here.

Week 1 Session 2

Born twice

Looking back

Do you know anyone who is unwell, sad or lonely at the moment?

Ask God to make them feel better.

Some people spend their time helping people who are unwell, sad or lonely. Pray for them as well.

To talk about

Do you know anyone who is expecting a baby?

Do you know anyone who has just had a baby?

What is a newborn baby like?

How many times is a baby born?

To do

Have you seen any pictures of yourself as a baby? Ask if you can see them and compare them to how you are now.

If you haven't any pictures, ask the person who has known you the longest what you were like when you were younger.

Explore the Bible

> **Jesus answered, 'I am telling you the truth: no one can see the Kingdom of God without being born again.'**
>
> *John 3:3*

When you are born, it is about starting out. It's the beginning of your life—everything is new. When Jesus talks in this verse about being born again, he doesn't mean being physically born. He means that we need to be born to another new life—a new life in God's family, which this verse calls the kingdom of God.

Prayer jotter

What do you think God's family is like?
Draw it or write about it here.
Where are you in the family?

Spiritual birth

Looking back

Were you involved in anything in the day just gone that would have made God sad? Think quietly to yourself and then say sorry to him.

To talk about

Think about the wind.

What does it do? How do you know if it is a windy day? Can you see the wind itself or only what it does?

Can you hear the wind itself or only what it does to noisy things?

To do

Which of these things needs the wind to make it work properly?

The Father's love

Looking back

Think about the people you love.

What do you love about them?

Thank God for them.

To talk about

How do you show that you love someone?

In what ways might fathers show that they love their children? Are there some things some fathers do that aren't very loving?

To do

Here are some ways to show love.

Choose your favourite ideas and draw a circle round them.

Explore the Bible

> **See how much the Father has loved us! His love is so great that we are called God's children.**
>
> *1 John 3:1*

Not every human father is loving all the time. You may know someone (it might be you) whose father is not very loving at all. This makes God sad. God is the best father we could ever imagine. He is better even than the best dad we know. His love for you is so amazing—he is your heavenly father.

Prayer jotter

Think of everything a good dad would do.

Think of the things God does for you.

Is there anything God does that a human dad could do?

Using words or pictures, thank God for being an amazing father.

All change!

Looking back

Is there anything you've heard about around the world that is making people sad, or hurting them?

Pray that God will be with them and that the people in charge will be wise in their actions.

To talk about

What is different between what you do now and what you did as a baby?

How do you eat now? How did the 'baby-you' eat? How do you get dressed? How do you move about?

To do

Draw a line between the baby-way and the child-way of doing things.

Explore the Bible

> **None of those who are children of God continue to sin, for God's very nature is in them; and because God is their Father, they cannot continue to sin.**
>
> *1 John 3:9*

When we grow up, we change and do new things. We will never go back to being a baby, drinking milk from a bottle or wearing nappies. When we are God's children—members of his family—we change. We no longer want to do some of the wrong things we used to do—we no longer sin. This is because we have changed inside. God's Holy Spirit is in us.

Prayer jotter

Sometimes, not sinning is very hard. Sometimes we do wrong things. This doesn't mean that God throws us out of his family. Rather, if we are sorry, he forgives us.

Ask God to help you say sorry and to try hard to live as his child.

After Jesus had returned to be with God in heaven, he wanted us to have someone to help us live a life pleasing to God. He promised us a helper, God's Holy Spirit, who comes to show us about God. He is the best helper there is, always knowing what we need help with.

To do

Circle the helpful things shown here.

Prayer jotter

God's Holy Spirit is always with us. He has been sent by Jesus to help us.

Has anything been happening to you recently that you need help with?

Ask Jesus to be with you through the Holy Spirit. Draw or write about it here.

Prayer jotter

What change would help you? Talk to God about it and draw the fire of the Holy Spirit. Think about how God's Holy Spirit might be like fire and heat which changes things.

God's promises

Looking back

God gets sad when we're mean or when we tell lies or make fun of others.

Is there anything you've done that you should say sorry for?

To do

At the beginning of the Bible is the story of Noah. Noah listened to God and built an ark to keep his family and the animals safe when it rained so hard that everything was flooded.

After the flood, God told Noah that he would put a rainbow in the sky so that God and people would remember the promises that God made. You can read about this in Genesis 9:11–15.

Colour this rainbow.

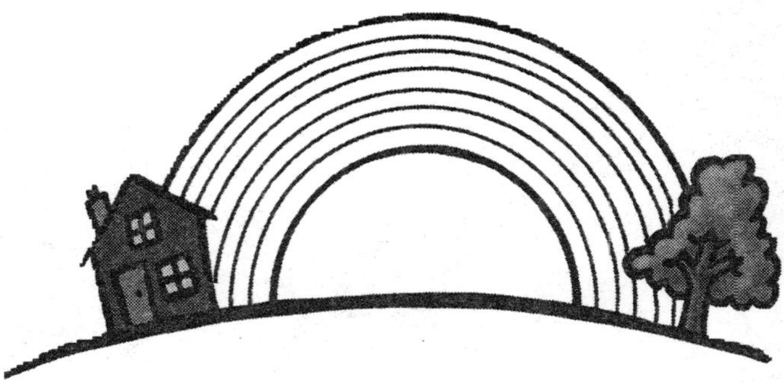

To talk about

Do you ever make promises?

What was the last promise that you made?

Have you ever broken a promise? Has anyone broken a promise that they made to you? How did that feel? Do you think that God would ever break a promise?

Explore the Bible

> **Then Peter stood up and in a loud voice began to speak to the crowd. 'This is what the prophet Joel spoke about: "This is what I will do in the last days, God says: I will pour out my Spirit on everyone."'**
>
> *Acts 2:14, 16–17*

God promises that he will send his Holy Spirit to everyone. We know that God keeps his promises. Promising not to flood the whole earth is just one promise of many that we find in the Bible.

Hundreds of years before Peter stood up to speak on that first day of Pentecost, the prophet Joel had told people about one of God's promises. This promise came true on the day of Pentecost.

Prayer jotter

God promises to be with us all the time. Joshua 1:5 says, 'I will always be with you; I will never abandon you.'

Sometimes we feel close to God and sometimes we feel far away. But we can rely on God's promises always. Write or draw about God's promises to you.

Owned by God

Looking back

What do you most love doing?

Thank God that you can do it. Ask him to help you to keep doing it.

To talk about

When you go shopping, how do you recognize the people who work in the shop?

If you found a lost dog or cat, what would you look for to help you know where to take it?

Do you have a mark on things you take to school to show they are yours? What happens if you lose them?

To do

Match up the lost thing with its owner.

Explore the Bible

It is God himself who has set us apart, who has placed his mark of ownership upon us, and who has given us the Holy Spirit in our hearts as the guarantee of all that he has in store for us.

2 Corinthians 1:21–22

God's Holy Spirit in our hearts is like a name tag in a jumper that says, 'I belong to God.' This might seem strange if we can't see or touch the Holy Spirit. Remember, though, that—like the wind—the Holy Spirit can't be seen, but what he does in people can. Your actions, helped by the Holy Spirit, are what show other people that you belong to God.

Prayer jotter

I belong to God. Isn't that amazing!

The creator father of the whole world is our owner! Do you think he looks after what is his?

Pray a 'thank you' to God and write or draw about belonging to God.

God's fruit

Looking back

What is the most beautiful thing you know? Thank God for why you like it.

Who is the most beautiful person you know? Thank God for why you like him or her.

God thinks you're beautiful. Say thanks for that, too!

To talk about

Do you have a favourite fruit or vegetable? Is it grown in this country? Does it grow on trees or in the ground?

Some fruits or vegetables have very special tastes. Does your favourite have a special flavour? Do you recognize it? Even mixed up with other flavours?

To do

Get someone to help you with a taste test. Get some different-flavour drinks or different-flavour crisps. Taste each flavour blindfolded. Can you recognize your favourite? Can you name each flavour?

Explore the Bible

But the Spirit produces love, joy, peace, patience, kindness, goodness, faithfulness, humility, and self-control.

Galatians 5:22–23

The Holy Spirit in us produces a special kind of fruit. Just as the pear tree grows pears and a banana tree has bananas, we, as God's tree, produce God's fruit.

These things in us make us have a distinct 'God-fruit' flavour.

The list of things in today's Bible verse are often called the 'fruit of the Spirit'.

Prayer jotter

Draw the tree of the Spirit, with the different things as its fruits.

Ask God to help you to have those fruits in your life through the Holy Spirit.

God's rules

Looking back

Think about school.

Thank God for something really good.

Ask him to help with something not so good.

To talk about

What rules do you have at school? How easy are they to live by? What happens if you don't live by the rules?

Do you have rules at home? What are they? Are you always happy to live by them?

To do

Play a game of 'Simon Says'. One person has to ask you to do something and you do it only if they say 'Simon says' first. You have to try to catch each other out by telling them to do something without saying 'Simon says' first!

Explore the Bible

The Spirit has given us life; he must also control our lives. We must not be proud or irritate one another or be jealous of one another.

Galatians 5:25–26

With God's Holy Spirit in our lives, we can start a new life. This new life with God is the best life we can have.

God has set some rules to help us live this new and better life. God's rules are about loving God and loving others. The Holy Spirit helps us to live by God's rules.

Prayer jotter

Is there anything hard about living life according to God's rules?

Write a prayer or draw about one thing you find hard.

Ask God's Holy Spirit to help you.

Promises, promises

Looking back

What is your favourite food? God created so many different tastes!

Thank him for your food today.

To talk about

What do people do to show that they mean what they say? Do they promise? Shake hands? Sign their name? When does this happen? Where?

Have you ever agreed to something and had to do something to prove you would do it?

Explore the Bible

So John appeared in the desert, baptizing and preaching. 'Turn away from your sins and be baptized,' he told the people, 'and God will forgive your sins.'

Mark 1:4

God wants us to live without sin, without doing things that hurt others and God. The man in this verse, John, came and told people that God wanted them to stop doing wrong things. He also asked them to do something to show that they meant to stop sinning. He asked them to be baptized.

John says that God will forgive us if we turn away from our sins. When God forgives, he completely takes away and forgets the wrong. We can then also forget it.

To do

Have you ever seen a baptism? Sometimes children and babies are baptized in a font.

Sometimes adults are baptized in a baptistry.

Both use water.

Over the next few sessions we will find out more about baptism.

Prayer jotter

Using words or pictures, thank God for his forgiveness.

Work in progress

Looking back

Think of all the things you do in water.

Thank God that you have water. Pray for people who don't have it.

To do

What do these signs mean? What is happening?

To talk about

Can you remember seeing a sign that said something was happening? What was it?

Can you think of any signs that show others we are a friend of Jesus? Have you seen any badges, or car stickers or posters?

Explore the Bible

> **John said, 'The man who will come after me is much greater than I am. I baptize you with water, but he will baptize you with the Holy Spirit.'**
>
> *Mark 1:7–8*

In the last session, we learnt that baptism is something people do as a sign that they have turned towards God. Here, John tells us that although his baptism is with water (just like ours today), Jesus will give us another sign that we have turned towards God—the Holy Spirit.

Turning towards God isn't always simple! Sometimes we don't always live the way we know he wants us to. For some, baptism is a sign that we are trying to live a new life.

Prayer jotter

Can you design a sign to show that the Holy Spirit is with you?

Belonging

Looking back

Think about your family. Pray for anyone you think needs God with them especially at the moment.

To talk about

Can you think of all the things that you belong to—a team, a family, a library, school clubs?

What do you have to show that you belong?

To do

Can you match these things? Which belongs to which?

Explore the Bible

> **Not long afterwards Jesus was baptized by John in the Jordan. As soon as Jesus came up out of the water, he saw heaven opening and the Spirit coming down on him like a dove. And a voice came from heaven, 'You are my own dear Son. I am pleased with you.'**
>
> *Mark 1:9–11*

When Jesus was baptized, something amazing happened. He was baptized in a river in Israel, the Jordan, and at the same time something like a dove came and alighted on him. That was the Holy Spirit coming. Then a voice from heaven told everyone in a clear voice, 'This is my Son.' Everyone knew who Jesus belonged to!

Baptism is a sign that we belong to someone. When we are baptized, it shows that we belong to God's family. Don't forget, though—God promises that everyone who loves him is in his family—baptized or not.

Prayer jotter

Write or draw about Jesus' baptism here.

Newness of life

Looking back

What is your favourite place? Imagine you are there.

Thank God for what you see in your imagination.

To talk about

What happens to a caterpillar when it comes out of its cocoon?

What happens to an acorn when you plant it?

What happens to a ball of wool when you knit with it?

All of them are transformed into something new. Can you think of any other examples?

To do

Match up the transformed objects.

Explore the Bible

> **By our baptism, then, we were buried with him and shared his death, in order that, just as Christ was raised from death by the glorious power of the Father, so also we might live a new life.**
>
> *Romans 6:4*

When the church first started, a man named Paul wrote a letter to help the Christians in Rome to get on together, and this verse is from that letter.

When people get baptized, a real transformation happens. Just as a caterpillar changes into a butterfly, so we too become different, with God's life inside us.

Paul explains how baptism is a way of showing this. When Jesus died and rose again, he promised to be with us all the time, so in baptism we are with him in everything we do.

Because Jesus really died and rose again, our sins really have been forgiven, so we really can live a new life. Baptism is a sign of our new 'forgiven' life. Wow!

Prayer jotter

Thank God that we can be changed by Jesus. Write or draw something you have learnt from this session.

Clothed with Jesus

Looking back

Sometimes we say things that we know we shouldn't say. Sometimes words come out that are mean or nasty.

This upsets God. It's good to say sorry to God.

To talk about

Have you ever played a game in which you dress up?

Have you got a dressing-up box at home or school?

Who do you like to become when you dress up?

Explore the Bible

> **You were baptized into union with Christ, and now you are clothed, so to speak, with the life of Christ himself.**
>
> *Galatians 3:27*

Do you remember the transformation we thought about in the last session?

Jesus forgives us right inside—we are transformed. Because the inside changes, the outside changes too—that is, the things we do and say.

When we dress up, it's like becoming a different person on the outside. But Jesus changes us from the inside. So we are truly changed. We become a new person, who, in baptism, puts on the life of Jesus, just like putting on new clothes.

To do

When some children are baptized, they wear special clothes, often a white gown. In many countries, adults also put on white clothes after they are baptized.

Try to find someone to talk to who can either show you some baptism clothes (it might be your gown) or show you a picture.

Prayer jotter

When we dress up, we don't change inside.

When we are baptized, Jesus changes us from the inside. He comes especially close to us and helps us stay especially close to him. Thank Jesus for that now.

Week 3
Session 6

Join the family

Looking back

How far back can you remember? Days, weeks or years? God has been with you even longer. Thank him for that.

To talk about

Think about your church and how many different people there are there. They have different hair colours, different heights, different nationalities and different ages. Think of the people who make you laugh, and all your friends there. Everyone is different and everyone belongs to the family.

Explore the Bible

There is one Lord, one faith, one baptism; there is one God and Father of all, who is Lord of all, works through all, and is in all.

Ephesians 4:5–6

All around the world there are millions of people joining God's family. There are more joining each second, even when you're asleep! That's amazing! Think of all those different people: some short, some tall, some fat, some thin, some old and some young, as many as you can think of. But this Bible verse reminds us that we, with them, all belong to the same God and we all belong to each other. When we are baptized, we also belong to the church family.

To do

Here are some blank faces. See if you can fill in the faces to look like the people you know at your church.

Prayer jotter

Thank God that you belong to such a huge family all the way round the world. See how many different people from God's family you can draw.

God's people

Looking back

Think of something new you learnt in the day just gone.

Thank God for it. Thank God for the person who taught you.

To talk about

Look around your room. What can you see that was made to do one special job? For example, a clock tells the time—it's no use for mowing a lawn or doing the washing-up.

Have you ever tried to use something that was made for one job to do something else? Did it work?

To do

Here are some tools. Which have one job and which have many?

Explore the Bible

> **'I will make you my own people, and I will be your God. You will know that I am the Lord your God when I set you free from slavery in Egypt.'**
>
> *Exodus 6:7*

When God made people, he made them with one special job. That was to belong to God and worship only him. Unfortunately God's people in the Old Testament were being kept as slaves in Egypt and couldn't worship God. But God promised that soon they would be free to belong to him again.

Prayer jotter

We live in a country where we are free to worship God. Some Christians in the world are put in prison for worshipping God. Draw them here and pray that God will be with them.

Let them go!

Looking back

Think about what you did with your friends in the day just gone.

Was it good? Fun? Exciting? Silly? Tell God about it and thank him for the good things.

To talk about

During most days we hear lots of instructions—'get dressed', 'go out to play', or 'eat your dinner'.

Think about what instructions you have heard today. Have you obeyed them all? Are there any instructions that you wouldn't obey?

To do

Here are people who give us instructions. What might they be saying?

Explore the Bible

Then the Lord said to Moses, 'Go and tell the king of Egypt that he must let the Israelites leave his land.'

Exodus 6:10–11

There are some people whose instructions we would always obey. There are also people who might not make us act immediately. Can you imagine God giving an instruction as clear as this? He wanted his people (the Israelites) to be allowed to leave Egypt so that they could worship him. What do you think the king did?

Prayer jotter

Moses listened to God and obeyed his instruction to go and tell the king what God wanted. God still tells people things today. How do you think he does this? Ask God to help you to hear him.

Not listening

Looking back

How many types of animal can you think of? God made them all!

Thank our creative God for all the colours, shapes and sizes in animals.

To talk about

Have you ever been ignored? What does it feel like?

Is there ever a good time to ignore someone? Who should we never ignore?

To do

Here are some signs we shouldn't ignore. Why not?

Explore the Bible

The king, however, remained stubborn and, just as the Lord had said, the king would not listen to Moses and Aaron.

Exodus 7:13

The king of Egypt was ignoring Moses. However much Moses and his brother Aaron explained and pleaded, he wouldn't listen. This instruction was from God. God wanted his people to be free to worship him. But the king ignored Moses. How would God make himself heard?

Prayer jotter

Do you think that God would ever ignore you? You can tell him anything. Tell him about your day in words or pictures.

Set free!

Looking back

What colour did you wear today? What's your favourite colour?

God made you to like, but also dislike, many things. He is an amazing maker! Praise him!

To talk about

Have you ever been punished for something you did? What was that like? Was it right that you were told off?

Have you ever been punished unfairly? Why? When someone tells you off, have they usually warned you before?

Explore the Bible

The Lord said to Moses, 'I will send only one more punishment on the king of Egypt and his people. After that he will let you leave.'

Exodus 11:1

God had asked the king of Egypt for the people to be set free. When the king wouldn't listen, God sent many warnings to show that he must be obeyed.

Egypt had already been overrun with frogs, gnats and flies, and locusts eating all their crops, as some of the warnings. God's final warning was the worst of all, because God really wanted his people to be set free. Finally the king had to listen.

To do

Here are some 'telling off' warnings you might have heard. Match the sentences and then finish the remaining sentence.

• 'If you don't hurry up in the bath, I'll...'	...switch off the TV
• If you don't go to bed now, I'll...	...pull the plug out
• 'If you don't stop annoying your sister, I'll...'	...not let you have a story

• 'If you don't finish your dinner, I'll...'

Prayer jotter

Often when we are asked to obey an instruction, it is because it is what is best for us. It isn't always easy to understand this, but we don't have to understand everything. Tell God about the things you don't understand.

Surprise

Looking back

Sometimes we do things without thinking—and end up hurting someone.

It might be an accident or it might be because we didn't care. Say sorry to God if this has happened to you and pray that he will help you to care for people.

To talk about

Do you like surprises? What was the last surprise you had?

Why did it surprise you?

What is the most unexpected thing you have ever seen? Was it a shock?

To do

Which of these things would be unexpected or a surprise? Why?

Explore the Bible

Moses held out his hand over the sea, and the Lord drove back the sea with a strong east wind. It blew all night and turned the sea into dry land. The water was divided, and the Israelites went through the sea on dry ground, with walls of water on both sides.

Exodus 14:21–22

God's people were escaping from slavery in Egypt. God did something unexpected to help them to escape. In order to let them cross the sea, he did not get them boats. Instead he divided the water through the middle so they could walk across on dry land. Can you imagine that? Wow!

Prayer jotter

Dividing the sea is amazing—we would have been surprised if we'd been there.

However, we should expect the unexpected from God! He is the Lord God of the whole world!

Praise God that he is surprising and draw something you have learnt from this session.

Week 4
Session 6

Power of God

Looking back

Pray for God to be with people who are ill in hospital. Ask him to help doctors and nurses to make them better.

To talk about

Who do you think is amazing? A footballer? A pop star? Your mum or dad? A teacher?

Why do you think they're amazing?

What is the most amazing thing they've done?

To do

People like being told they are amazing. Why not write a letter telling someone that you think they are amazing? If you want, you could also draw a picture of them doing something amazing.

Explore the Bible

The water returned and covered all the Egyptian army that had followed the Israelites into the sea; not one of them was left. But the Israelites walked through the sea on dry ground. When the Israelites saw the great power of the Lord, they stood in awe of the Lord.

Exodus 14:28–29, 31

The Israelites were amazed at what God had done. He had pulled back the water in the sea to make a path for the people to walk through to freedom. Then he let the water back all over the chasing army, to protect his people. And all because he cared so much about them. What a great God!

Prayer jotter

Is there one thing that you find totally amazing about God? Draw or write about it here and tell him he's amazing.

Can you see Jesus?

Looking back

Some people are homeless. They are usually poor and hungry, too.

Pray for the people who help them. Pray that those without homes might be made more comfortable.

To talk about

Have you ever had to imagine what something is like because you haven't seen it for real? How about where you are going on holiday? Or a friend's new house?

How easy is it to think about something we haven't seen or touched for real? If you have difficulties with your eyes, this might be easier.

To do

Play a feely-touchy game. Close your eyes or wear a blindfold and get someone else to give you something to feel—can you guess what it is? Try again with something else. Take turns at being the guesser.

Explore the Bible

All of you are Christ's body, and each one is a part of it.

1 Corinthians 12:27

Sometimes it's hard for us to imagine Jesus being alive and with us today because we can't actually see him. However, this Bible verse tells us that Jesus does still have a body here—it's us! How can that be? When the Bible talks of Christ's body, it is talking about the church—God's people.

Prayer jotter

Most people have an idea of what God looks like in their imagination. How about you?

See if you can draw it here or, if you prefer, use words to describe what you see in your imagination.

Week 5
Session 2

All different

Looking back

How many different flowers do you know? How many different colours do they have? God made them all! Tell him he is a clever creator!

To talk about

Do you like finding new things that your body can do? Can you do a forward roll? A handstand? Can you run fast? Do you know anyone who runs faster?

To do

With someone else, try to find something you can do that they can't.

Try rolling your tongue up or going cross-eyed. Now try the other way round. What can they do that you can't?

Explore the Bible

> **Christ is like a single body, which has many parts; it is still one body, even though it is made of different parts.**
>
> *1 Corinthians 12:12*

Think about the people at your church. Does everyone look exactly the same? Can everyone play an instrument or lead the singing? Does everyone do the same things to help out? Although we do lots of different things in church, we are all doing them for Jesus. Just as you, as one person, can do lots of different things, so the people in church doing different things actually work like one person. They are all doing it for Jesus.

Prayer jotter

Sometimes, thinking about what we can and cannot do makes us sad because we really want to be able to do something we can't.

God cares about what we want.

Tell him about it, either with pictures or words.

Different jobs

Looking back

What did you do in school the last time you were there? Thank God for something brilliant! Tell him about something not so good.

To talk about

Look at your hands. Try to think of at least ten things they do.

Now think of what your feet do. What do you do with your nose? Your eyes? Your elbows? Is there anything that you can do with your eyes that you can do with another part of your body?

To do

Match the pictures of things we use with the right part of the body.

Explore the Bible

If the foot were to say, 'Because I am not a hand, I don't belong to the body,' that would not keep it from being part of the body. As it is, however, God put every different part in the body just as he wanted it to be.

1 Corinthians 12:15 and 18

This verse explains more about the church being Christ's body. There have to be lots of different people at church who can do all sorts of different things, because there are so many different things to do as God's people. The important thing to remember is that each part is valuable and necessary in the church, just as we need each body part to do its special job.

Do you have any bit of your body that doesn't work as well as it could?

Maybe you have problems seeing, hearing, walking or writing. God promises that everyone belongs to his body, the church. We won't be left out.

Prayer jotter

Thank God that you belong to his body, and draw a picture of yourself here.

No one is weaker

Looking back

Think about the oldest people in your family. Pray that God will be with them and give them everything they need.

To talk about

Do you think that there is any part of your body that is unimportant? What about your little toe? What does that do? What about your third finger—it's not very strong, so why do we need it? Is there any body part that we don't use?

To do

These body parts might seem quite weak. But what couldn't we do without them?

Explore the Bible

We cannot do without the parts of the body that seem to be weaker. God himself has put the body together in such a way as to give greater honour to those parts that need it.

1 Corinthians 12:22 and 24

The church is like a body. Just as our body makes use of every part it has, the church uses every part it has. The parts of the church's body are its members, like you and me! No one is more valuable or useful—every part is needed.

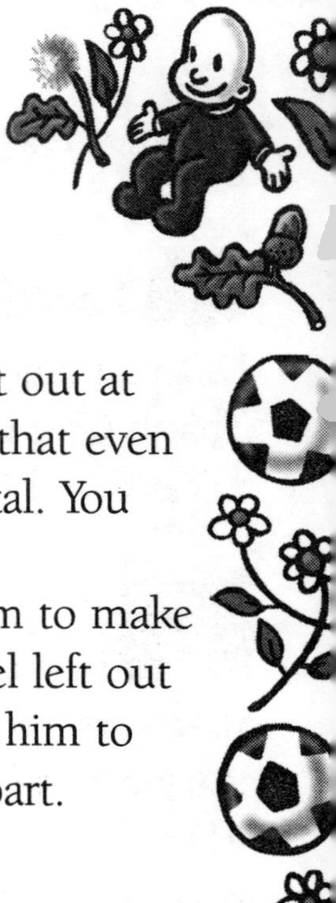

Prayer jotter

Do you ever feel small and left out at church? If you do, remember that even little bits on our bodies are vital. You are vital at church.

Tell God about it and ask him to make things change. If you don't feel left out at church, thank him and ask him to help you to help others take part.

Love and respect

Looking back

Did you enjoy your food in the day just gone? Thank God that you have food to eat. Pray for God to be with hungry people.

To talk about

Have you got a group of special friends? What are their names?

Do you know anyone else who has a group of special friends that you are not part of? Who are they? Do you ever feel left out? Do you think other people ever feel left out of your group of friends?

To do

Here are lots of different people in a group. Who should be together? Can you sort them out?

Explore the Bible

> **Love one another warmly as Christian brothers and sisters, and be eager to show respect for one another.**
>
> *Romans 12:10*

In a place called Rome, in Italy, there was a church with two different groups of people in it. They weren't very good at getting on together. A church leader called Paul wrote them a letter, telling them that because Jesus loved them all equally they should try to get on together. Just like we saw in the last session, he told them that they were one body and so they should try to love each other, because they were part of the same family.

Prayer jotter

Who do you find it difficult to get on with at church? Is there a group that you are left out of?

Ask God here to give you his special love for these people, so that you can love and respect them as if they were your family.

Work hard

Looking back

Think of something you think is amazing. Thank God that he made amazing things. Praise him that he made people to make amazing things.

To talk about

When you're at school, what is it that makes you work hard? To get good marks? So your teacher is happy?

Do you ever help out at home? What do you do? Why do you do that?

To do

Think of something helpful that you could do in each of these places.

Explore the Bible

Work hard and do not be lazy. Serve the Lord with a heart full of devotion.

Romans 12:11

When we are part of the church, we do what this Bible verse says. We work hard for many reasons—to help others, to make things happen properly, and to make things easier. Most of all, we do it because we belong to God's family. In a way we are helping him out and this pleases him.

Prayer jotter

What can you do to help out at church? Think about it now and draw a picture or write about yourself as part of God's family.